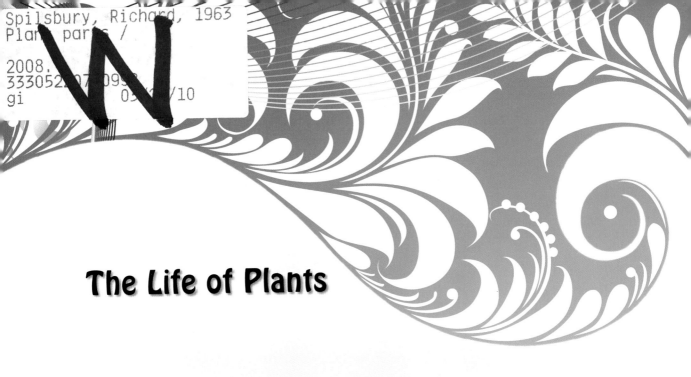

The Life of Plants

Plant Parts

Richard & Louise Spilsbury

Heinemann
LIBRARY

Chicago, Illinois

Customer Service 888-454-2279
Visit our website at www.heinemannraintree.com

Design: Victoria Bevan and Planman Technologies
Illustrations: Jeff Edwards
Printed and bound in China by CTPS

12 11 10 09 08
10 9 8 7 6 5 4 3 2 1

Library of Congress Cataloging-in-Publication Data
Spilsbury, Louise
Plant parts / Louise and Richard Spilsbury
    p. cm. -- (Life of Plants)
Includes bibliographical references (p.).
Summary: Describes the world of plants and the various parts of specific plants, such as flower, seed, roots, trunk, and more.
ISBN 978-1-4329-1499-8 (hbk)
ISBN 978-1-4329-1506-3 (pbk)
1. Plants--Juvenile literature. 2. Botany--Anatomy--Juvenile literature. [1. Plants. 2. Plant physiology.] I. Spilsbury, Richard, 1963- II. Title. III Series.
    QK49 .S735 2002
    580--dc21

                              2001008302

Acknowledgments
The publishers would like to thank the following for permission to reproduce photographs: ©Ardea p. **15t** (Steve Hopkin); ©Corbis pp. **4**, **11b**, **27**, **37**; ©FLPA pp. **13**, **21**; ©Garden matters p. **17**; ©Getty Images/Axiom Photographic Agency p. **19** (Naki Kouyioumtzis); ©Getty Images/PhotoDisc p. **18b**; ©Holt Studios pp. **5**, **7**, **8**, **10**, **12**, **14**, **16**, **22**, **25**, **28**, **29**, **31**, **35**, **38**; ©Oxford Scientific Films pp. **4**, **26**, **32**, **33**, **39**; ©Science Photo Library pp. **9** (Dr. Jeremy Burgess), **24**, **34** Andrew Syred p. **30**, Claude Nurisany and Marie Perennou p. **19**, Will and Deni McIntyre p. **36**; ©Science Photo Library p. **37** (Dr. Keith Wheeler).

Cover photograph of a Calypson orchid reproduced with permission of NHPA/David Middleton.

The publishers would like to thank Andrew Solway and Ann Fullick for their assistance in the preparation of this book.

Every effort has been made to contact copyright holders of any material reproduced in this book. Any omissions will be rectified in subsequent printings if notice is given to the publishers.

Disclaimer

Contents

Any words appearing in the text in bold, **like this**, are explained in the glossary.

A plant may be called different things in different countries, so every type of plant has a Latin name that can be recognized anywhere in the world. Latin names are made of two words: the first is the genus (general group) a plant belongs to and the second is its species (specific) name. Latin plant names are given in parentheses throughout this book.

Looking at Plants

There is a bewildering variety of plants in the world. They range from tiny, barely visible plants that you might step on without noticing as you walk on a mountain, to huge cacti in a hot, sandy desert. Yet even though plants all over the world look so incredibly different, most of them are made up of the same basic parts.

Each part of a plant has a job to do. Plants, like other **organisms**, need food to live, grow, and repair themselves. Animals eat plants, or they eat other animals that eat plants.

Plants all over

Scientists estimate that there are more than 300,000 species of plants in the world, of which around 260,000 are flowering plants. However, no one knows for sure. Many species of plants have not yet been discovered. If we do not protect plant **habitats**, some of them will become extinct (die out) before they have ever been classified.

All flowering plants—the most common kind of plant—have parts called **roots**, **stems**, **leaves**, and **flowers**.

A job to do

Plants make their own food by a special process called **photosynthesis**, using sunlight, water, and **carbon dioxide**. Some parts of the plant collect these ingredients, and other parts put them together to make food.

Like other organisms, plants also need to **reproduce**. They reproduce so that their **species** can survive after their death. Plants have special parts that allow them to reproduce when the time is right.

Different plant parts all have a particular job to do, even though they may look very different on each kind of plant.

Plant building blocks

All organisms are made up of tiny living parts called **cells**. They are so small you can usually only see them using a microscope. Not all plant cells are the same. Different groups of cells form different plant parts, and they help that part do its job. Most plant cells look like minuscule, water-filled balloons, with a tiny, rigid cell wall (see right). Plant cells have these walls, but animal cells do not.

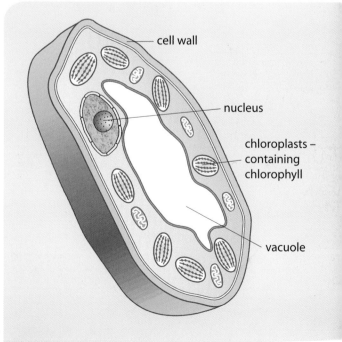

cell wall

nucleus

chloroplasts – containing chlorophyll

vacuole

Leaves

Leaves come in many different sizes, shapes, and arrangements. Leaf shapes are one of the clues that can tell you what type of plant you are looking at. For example, the leaves of the banana plant are flat, wide, and can be several feet long. The leaves of the aloe plant are thick with tough skins, but have jelly-like insides.

Leaves can be oval, circular, star-shaped, or heart-shaped. Some leaves, such as spinach, have smooth, rounded edges, but others, such as sweet chestnut (*Castanea sativa*), have jagged edges. Most leaves are made up of one piece, like the maple (*Acer*). Others, such as those on the ash (*Fraxinus*), are made up of smaller leaves, called "leaflets," all joined to a central **stalk**.

World's longest leaves

The raffia palm (*Raphia farinifera*) has the longest leaves of all palm trees. Its leaves grow up to 66 feet (20 meters) long, which is about the same as two buses parked end to end!

These photos give you an idea of the huge variety of leaf shapes and colors found on plants around the world.

Leaf structure

Even though leaves look very different, they usually have the same parts. The flat part of a leaf is called the **blade**. Leaf blades grow from the **stem** on a stalk, although some grow straight out of the stem. The leaf stalk (called the **petiole**) can bend so that the leaf does not snap off the plant if it is hit by a gust of wind.

The petiole is attached to a **midrib**, which runs along the center of the leaf blade. On plants such as the beech (*Fagus*), leaf **veins** branch off from this central midrib. On other plants, such as buffalo grass (*Buchloe dactyloides*), the leaf veins are all lined up from bottom to top. The veins form a network of tubes that connect the leaf to all the other parts of the plant. Water taken in by the **roots** of the plant moves to the leaves through these tubes. A sugary liquid (**sap**) that carries food from the leaves to other parts of the plant also travels through them.

The veins act a bit like the bones in our bodies. They help keep the leaf blade stiff and flat. If you see a dead leaf rotting under a tree or bush, you can see the leaf skeleton (network of veins) very easily. The leaf skeleton takes longer to rot than the leaf blade because it is made of tougher **cells**.

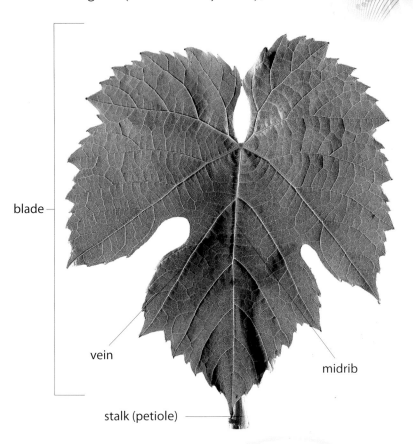

blade

vein

midrib

stalk (petiole)

Different plants have leaves with different vein patterns. If you hold a vine leaf, like this one, up to the light, you should be able to see the network of veins that run through it.

Looking at Leaves

Leaves are one of the most important parts of any plant. Leaves help plants get the sunlight and **carbon dioxide** that they need to make their own food, which they do in a process called **photosynthesis**. In photosynthesis, plants use the **energy** from sunlight to combine the carbon dioxide and water, and turn them into energy-rich foods.

To get light, many leaves are large and flat, because that is the best shape for absorbing (soaking up) lots of light. Bigger plants need more food to keep them going than smaller plants, so they often have several big leaves or thousands of small ones in order to make enough.

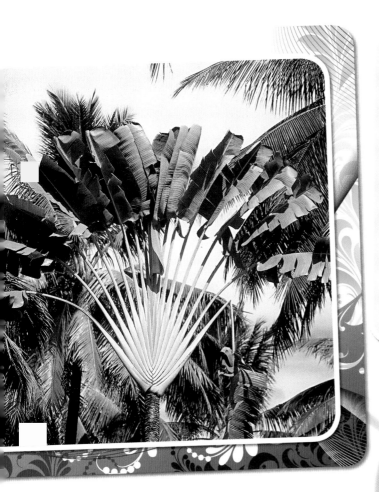

Light-catching leaves

Have you ever wondered why leaves grow where they do on plants? They are often positioned high up on a **stem** to receive as much light as possible. Stems and **stalks** hold the leaves out so they can get a share of the light. Sometimes leaves grow alternately— first one side of the stem and then the other, a bit farther up. Some grow in a spiral around the stem or opposite each other, in pairs from the same point on the stem.

The leaves on this banana fan palm are arranged so that they don't overlap each other. That way each leaf gets as much light as it can.

Why are leaves green?

Most leaves are green. This is because they contain a green substance called **chlorophyll**. Chlorophyll is essential for photosynthesis. The leaves of some plants are different colors, such as reddish purple in copper beech (*Fagus purpurea*). Their leaves still contain chlorophyll, but another **pigment**, the red color, is stronger.

Close up!

Take a good, close look at a leaf. The upper side of the leaf is different from the underside. It often has a waxier, thicker surface than the underside. Most photosynthesis happens in the **cells** of the leaf's upper side, so this is the side that always faces the sun. Warmth from the sun **evaporates** water inside the leaf, so the waxy coat reduces the amount of water the leaf loses.

Under the microscope

Stomata

On the underside of a leaf there are lots of little holes called **stomata**. These are so small that they can only be seen through a microscope. There may be thousands of stomata in every square inch of the leaf's surface. The plant opens its stomata to take in the air it needs for photosynthesis. It can also close them when it is hot, to stop too much water from evaporating.

Needles and Spines

Some people find it hard to believe that the long, thin needles of a pine tree and the sharp spines of a cactus plant are really different types of **leaves**. They *are* leaves, and they grow in these special shapes to help the plants they grow on to survive.

Pine trees are **coniferous**. They are able to survive cold weather, when water in the ground may be locked up in ice, because of the form of their leaves. If you look closely at pine needles, you will see that they have a groove on the underside. The leaf's **stomata** are inside the groove. This gives them shelter from wintry winds that might **evaporate** water from inside the leaf. A thick, waxy coating on the needles gives them extra protection.

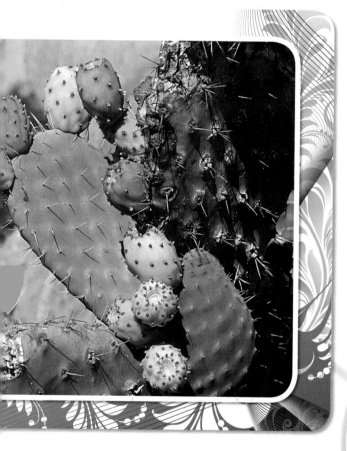

Most cacti live in hot, dry deserts. Cactus spines are very thin leaves. Like needles, they lose very little water by evaporation. Unlike conifers, which carry out **photosynthesis** in their green needles, cacti plants make their food in their thick **stems**. The spines that come straight out of the stem are often brown. The stems are green because they contain the **chlorophyll** necessary for photosynthesis.

Cactus spines have many uses! The sharp spines on this cactus help to defend it from animals that want to eat the watery flesh inside its stem.

Types of needles

Some needles, such as white cedar (*Thuja occidentalis*), are short, soft, and flat like scales. Other needles, such as Eastern white pine (*Pinus strobus*), are around 4 inches (10 centimeters) long and grow in groups of five. Juniper (*Juniperus*) needles grow in groups of three. The leaves of the monkey-puzzle tree (*Araucaria araucana*) are tough and triangular, and grow in spirals along its branches. They are very sharp in order to protect the tree's **cones** from being eaten by animals.

These are the needles of a conifer tree.

Deciduous and coniferous leaves

The broad, flat leaves of **deciduous** trees such as common beech (*Fagus sylvatica*) would be damaged by cold winter weather. So, they shed their leaves in the fall and grow new ones in the spring, when the weather is warmer. In winter, their branches are bare.

Coniferous trees, such as the Scots pine in the picture, are those that have cones and needle-like leaves, such as common spruce (*Picea abies*) or Douglas fir (*Pseudotsuga menziesii*). Their tough, thick, and waxy leaves can survive harsh winter weather. Such trees do not need to shed all their leaves in the fall. They drop some old leaves and grow some new leaves throughout the year. Some people call such trees evergreens because they always look green.

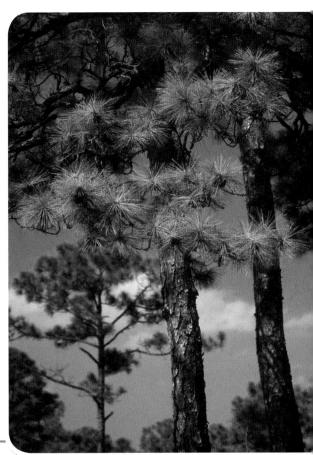

Buds

When new **leaves** suddenly appear on trees in spring on a **deciduous** tree, where do they come from? The answer is from tiny packages called **buds**. If you look at a tree in winter, the buds are already there, at the ends and along the lengths of the twigs and branches.

A deciduous tree stops or slows down growth in winter, but its buds are ready to quickly start growing again in spring. Inside the buds, tiny leaves wait, folded neatly in their protective case. When warmth and light from spring sunshine hits the buds, they begin to grow and swell until they burst open and the leaves emerge. Once the leaves are out, they can start to make food for the tree.

Different buds

Different plants have different types of buds. The horse chestnut tree (*Aesculus hippocastanum*) has large, sticky buds. The ash tree (*Fraxinus excelsior*) has small buds that are as black as ash from a dead fire. The buds of the lily-flowered magnolia tree (*Magnolia liliiflora*) are covered in soft, thick fur. In winter, when there are no leaves to help you identify a tree, a good look at the buds can help you figure out what it is.

The buds on a horse chestnut tree are sticky in order to discourage insects from eating them.

Flower buds

Flowers can seem to appear on a plant as if by magic. One day they are not there—and the next they are. Flowers are able to appear so swiftly, when the conditions are right, because they are already formed, in miniature, inside buds. Covers called **sepals** protect the fragile, folded young flower **petals** just inside the bud. After the sepals have opened, the petals grow and spread out of a flower bud rapidly. Some types of plants, such as tulips, produce only one flower, so they will grow only one bud. Others, such as apple trees, grow many flowers, which burst out of many small and tightly packed buds.

First, the bud of a tulip swells and grows. Then, the petals push their way out of the sepals into the light like these have.

Hibernating plants?

Most of us have heard of bears hibernating—but plants? **Bulbs** are like underground buds, and they allow certain plants to rest through winter when the cold weather could kill them. Onions are a well-known kind of bulb. Bulbs consist of layers of thick, fleshy leaves surrounding a central bud. A papery skin protects the whole bulb. In the fall the plant parts above ground die. The bulb survives the winter underground, waiting to grow new leaves and flowers from its bud in the warmth of the following spring.

Flowers

There is an immense variety of **flowers** in the world. Single flowers range in size from less than an inch to several feet across. Some are simple in shape and pattern, while others are incredibly complicated. Flowers may be blue, yellow, white, red, or purple, or a combination of colors. Flowers across the world may all look very different, but the basic parts of a flower are the same.

Flowers grow out of **buds**. The swollen end of the flower nearest the **stem** is called a **receptacle**. The other parts of the flower are above this. On the outside are the **sepals**, which protect the young, fragile flower parts as they develop. They often look like small green **leaves**. **Petals** are usually the largest and most colorful part of a flower.

The reproductive parts

A flower is the headquarters of the plant's **reproductive** system. It is where the **seeds**, which may grow into new plants, are made. A flower contains male and female parts. The female parts are called the **carpel**. At the bottom is the **ovary**, which produces and holds the female **sex cells**. The **stamens** are the male parts. The **anthers**, at the top of each stamen, produce male sex cells, each of which is stored inside a protective **pollen** grain.

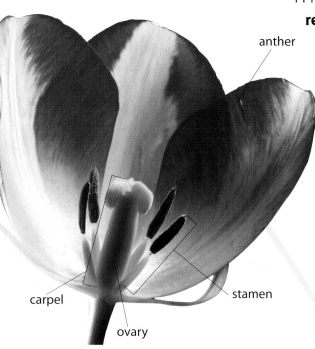

anther

carpel

ovary

stamen

This photo of a tulip shows the different parts of its flower.

How do flowers reproduce?

In order to produce a seed, a male sex cell must fuse with a female sex cell from the same plant or a different plant of the same **species**. This is called **fertilization**. To do this, pollen must move from an anther to an ovary. This movement is called **pollination**, and it often happens with the help of insects.

This is where the flower's petals and **nectary** come in handy. A nectary is a small sac at the bottom of a petal that contains sweet liquid called **nectar**. Insects visit flowers to feed on the nectar. Pollen from the anthers brushes onto their bodies. When they stop off at another flower, it rubs off again, hopefully onto the top of a carpel.

When the pollen grain lands at the top of a carpel, the male sex cell inside moves down into the ovary. It joins with the female cells, and a seed starts to grow.

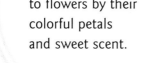

Insects are attracted to flowers by their colorful petals and sweet scent.

Awesome flowers

The largest single flower in the world is the rafflesia (see right). Once every 10 years it produces a foul-smelling flower that grows up to 3 feet (1 meter) wide and 15 pounds (7 kilograms) in weight. However, the titan arum is possibly even more spectacular. It produces a tower of tiny flowers, which can be 10 feet (3 meters) high!

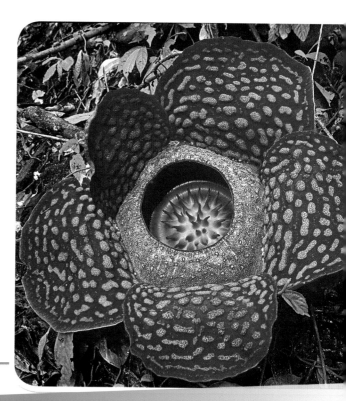

Types of Flowers

Different **species** of plants have different colors, shapes, and arrangements of **flowers**. Bluebells (*Scilla*) have **petals** that are joined together to form a bell. Violets (*Viola*) have petals of different shapes all on one flower. In clematis flowers, it is the **sepals** that are colorful, not the petals. In fuchsias, both the sepals and petals are brightly colored as a kind of double show to draw insects' attention to them. Sometimes the sepals and petals look exactly the same. This is common in lilies, for example.

In some flowers, such as sunflowers, dandelions, and daisies, the "petals" are not petals at all—each is part of a tiny flower called a floret. In sunflowers the center of the flower is made up of florets, too. The whole flower-like head (called an **inflorescence**) contains hundreds of separate flowers! Each floret is a flower in its own right because each is capable of making a **seed**.

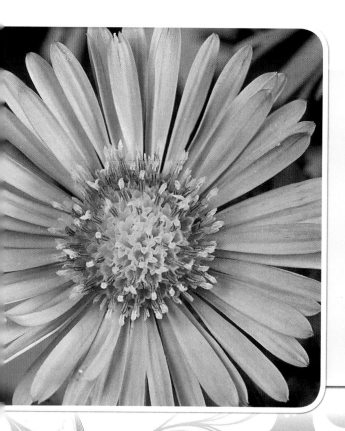

Flower tricks

Try this trick on your friends. Hold a daisy in your hand and ask them how many flowers you are holding. When they say one, you can surprise them with the fact that there are actually about 250. Pull a daisy into pieces and you will see that the daisy is not one flower, but many florets joined together. The yellow central part of the daisy is made up of many tiny, tube-shaped florets. On the edge of the daisy there are different florets, each with a pink petal on it.

Flower forms

Each species of plant always grows its flowers in a particular way. The way flowers are arranged on a plant is as important for identifying them as the color or size of their petals.

Some plants, such as the tulip or crocus, grow a single flower out of the end of a single **stem**. Others, such as the scabious (*Scabiosa*), grow lots of flowers, each one often developing and opening at different times and on different stems. The flowers of some plants grow in spires or spikes. Foxglove (*Digitalis purpurea*) flowers grow on little **stalks** coming out of the stem. The flowers at the bottom usually look bigger than the ones at the top because they open first.

Other plants have flowers that grow in groups called **clusters**. Some have lots of small flowers on separate little stalks growing out of the top of the stem. Sometimes these flowers droop down, as in giant yellow cowslips (*Primula florindae*). In some plants, such as giant hogweed (*Heracleum*), many flowers all grow from the same point on the stalk. If the tiny flowers are raised up until they are almost at the same level together, they look a bit like an umbrella. In fact, the name for this shape of flower is an **umbel**.

The umbrella-like shape of an umbellifer, such as this giant hogweed, provides a helpful platform for insects to land on.

What Is a Fruit?

If someone asked you to name three fruits, chances are you would come up with suggestions like oranges, bananas, apples, or pears. But would you think of the "helicopters" (keys) on a sycamore or maple tree, or pea **pods**, or cucumber? In science, the word "fruit" means the part of a flowering plant in which **seeds** develop.

Fruits of different **species** can look very different, but they all share two important jobs: to protect developing seeds and to help move them away from the plant. Seeds start to develop if **pollination** has happened. When a plant has finished flowering, the **petals** on its **flowers** die and fall off the plant. The hollow part at the bottom of the flower, called the **ovary**, starts to swell. This is usually the part that slowly grows into a fruit.

After a tomato flower's petals fall from the plant, its ovary swells into a round green fruit. The tomato turns red when the seeds inside are ready.

"False fruits"

The true fruit of an apple tree is the core, because it is the ovary that holds the seeds. The fleshy part of the apple—the part we eat and think of as the fruit—is actually the swollen top of the flower stalk (the **receptacle**). The fleshy part has grown around the real fruit. Other "false fruits" like this include pears and rosehips.

Types of fruit

Some fruits are fleshy (soft and juicy). Fleshy fruits such as cherries or apricots have only one seed inside them, contained in a hard "stone." Other fleshy fruits such as melon, cucumber, or tomato have lots of seeds, scattered throughout the flesh or held in a central core. Blackberries and loganberries are compound fruits. Each seed is contained in its own package of sweet flesh, and lots of packages together form the compound fruit. Some plants, such as pumpkins, produce a few giant fruits. Other plants, such as elder, produce hundreds of small fruits called berries.

Dry fruits include the pods of soybeans, the seed capsules of poppies, and the winged seed cases of plant trees (*Platanus*). The dry fruit of the horse chestnut is hard and spiky in order to protect the seed inside from being eaten before it drops to the ground.

Tumbleweeds

Most plants produce fruit to ensure their seeds are **dispersed**. Tumbleweeds are different! The whole plant breaks off at the **root** and rolls away in the wind, scattering seeds as it goes. Tumbleweeds originally came from Russia, but now they are found in the United States and Australia. Each ripe tumbleweed can contain 250,000 seeds to be scattered over a wide area.

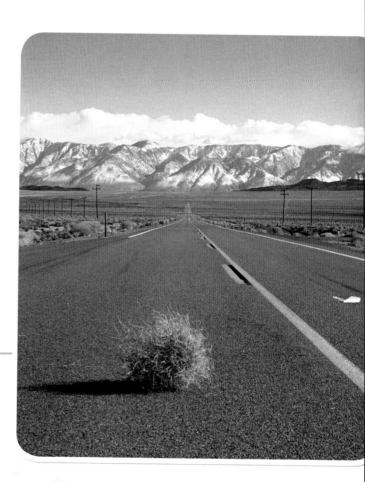

Why Do Plants Have Fruits?

One of the things a new young plant needs to grow well is space. It needs room to spread its **roots** and unfold its **leaves** into the light. If a seedling (young plant) tries to grow when it is too close to other plants, including its parent plant, it will have to compete for the things it needs. Plants cannot move, so how do they ensure that the **seeds** they produce end up somewhere new? The answer is fruit! Fruits protect the developing seeds, but also use clever ways to **disperse** (scatter) them.

Fruits come in different shapes, sizes, and forms, depending on the way they spread their seeds. Some plants use the wind, water, or animals to help disperse their seeds. Others have fruits that suddenly split or pop open, catapulting seeds away from the plant.

Fruits that are dispersed by the wind, water, or explosion are usually light and fairly small, like poppy seeds. Maple keys have wings so that they can spin away from their parent tree. Dandelion fruits have hairs that act like miniature parachutes when caught by the wind, taking them long distances in the air.

Some fruits, such as those of the alder tree, are dispersed by water. Alder trees grow by rivers, so their fruits drop into the water. Oil in the case around the alder seed helps it float until it lands somewhere that it might grow.

The dry fruits of the maple tree have two light, spreading wings. When they fall from the tree, their shape helps them to fall and spin in the air, carrying the seeds away from their parent plant.

Plants that use explosion to disperse their seeds have specially shaped fruits. Peapods twist and dry up when their seeds are fully developed. The twisting makes the two halves of the **pods** burst open, scattering the seeds around.

Animal assistance

The skins of many fruits are colorful and appealing, and the flesh is sweet and good to eat. This is no accident. When a bird or other animal is attracted to eat a fruit, it often swallows it whole—skin, flesh, and seeds. Later on, the seeds fall to the ground in the animal's droppings. Such seeds usually have extra-tough outer cases so that they are not damaged as they pass through the animal's digestive system. Animals also spit out seeds or drop partly eaten fruit far away from the plant on which the fruit grew.

The forbidden fruit

Durian is a type of spiky fruit weighing several pounds that grows in Southeast Asia. The skin of durian has a disgusting smell (like rotting fish), but its custard-like flesh is delicious to eat. Orangutans (see right) love to eat durians. The strong smell helps to direct them to the trees where the fruit grows.

In Singapore, people are not allowed to take durians in many taxis or on buses and airplanes because the smell is so unpleasant to most people!

Seeds

All flowering plants make **seeds**. Seeds come in a huge variety of sizes, shapes, and colors. Some seeds are so small they look like dust or grains of powder. The seeds of some **rain forest** orchids are so tiny that millions of their seeds would weigh less than 0.03 ounces (1 gram). At the other end of the scale, an individual seed on a coconut tree usually weighs more than 4 pounds (2 kilograms).

Seeds are like packages with tiny plants inside. Each seed contains what it needs to start growing into a new plant. Inside a seed there is an **embryo** (a partly developed plant or seedling) and a store of plant food. This food is used to keep the embryo alive while it is inside the seed, and to give it **energy** to **germinate**. Most seeds also need water, air, and the right temperature to germinate.

Most seeds store their food in special tiny **seed leaves**. The seed leaves also form the first **leaves** that emerge from the seed once it germinates. Some plants, such as maize, have only one seed leaf in their seeds. Others, such as fava beans, have two.

Seeds are like little packages. The seed coat keeps the embryo and seed leaves safe until the conditions are right for it to start to grow into a new plant.

Seed coats

The outer layer of a seed is called the **seed coat** and it does three important jobs. It protects the embryo from injury, perhaps when the seed drops from the plant. It also protects the food supply, stopping the food-rich seed leaves inside from being eaten by insects and other animals. The seed coat also stops the seed from losing water, and so prevents it from drying out completely.

Seeds and germination

Having an efficient seed coat is important because most seeds remain **dormant** rather than germinating right after they leave the parent plant. This rest period stops seeds from sprouting until the time is right. For example, many seeds remain dormant in cold winter months and germinate in the warmth of spring. Some seeds can survive for years, decades, or even centuries, before the conditions are right for them to germinate.

Ancient seeds

The seeds of the Arctic lupin (*Lupinus arcticus*) can survive for an incredibly long time. Arctic soil is very cold and acts like a freezer, preserving things buried in it. It has been reported that Arctic lupin seeds found in a frozen lemming burrow in the Yukon Territory of Canada were 10,000 years old. Scientists managed to germinate some of these ancient seeds within 48 hours!

When conditions are right, a seed will germinate. A **shoot** emerges from the seed and grows up to the light. The first root grows out of the seed and down into the soil.

Nuts

Hundreds of different shrubs and trees produce nuts, but what exactly are nuts? Nuts are actually types of **seeds**. They all have a hard or woody outer layer that forms what we call the shell. Inside the shell is the kernel.

The kernel is the seed, and it is also the part that animals, including us, like to eat. Kernels are usually rich in **protein** and **fat** or oil. These are the foods that the seed uses to stay alive. It also uses this food store to grow new **roots** and **shoots**, if it gets the chance to **germinate**. Most seeds need water for germination, but it is especially important for nuts. Nut shells are hard and tough, but water softens them so that they break apart more easily to release the seeds inside.

shell

kernel

Top seed

The prize for the biggest nut in the world goes to the coco-de-mer tree (*Lodoicoa maldivica*). Its huge seeds can weigh up to 44 pounds (20 kilograms) each, but they can float in the sea. The fibers around the shell trap air, and the inside of the nut is hollow. The nut floats between islands until it lands somewhere it can germinate.

Wild mammals, such as squirrels, which eat nuts like these, have strong teeth. They need them to crack open the nut's hard shell.

Nuts on the move

Just like other seeds, nuts are more likely to germinate if they do not have to compete for light, **nutrients**, and water with their parent plant. So, how do nuts move away from their parents? Before winter, animals such as chipmunks and squirrels gather nuts from trees. They eat some and bury the rest, often in open land. When winter comes and food is scarce, the chipmunk tries to find its food stores. However, just like us, chipmunks are forgetful, so they never find all the nuts. These forgotten seeds can grow into new trees in the spring, given the right conditions. If the chipmunk happens to bury the nuts deep enough, they will be protected by the soil until they are ready to germinate!

A hard nut to crack

Brazil nuts, as their name suggests, come from Brazil. In the Amazon **rain forest**, local people pick nuts from wild Brazil nut trees (*Bertholletia excelsa*) in the forest. They have to climb very tall trees to get them. The nuts are hidden inside hard wooden cases, which have to be smashed open. Inside, the seeds are protected in smaller and very hard shells. The Brazil nut case in the photo has been cut in half to show the white nuts inside their shells. Brazil nuts often have to hang around a long time before conditions are right for them to germinate.

Cones

Conifer trees do not grow **flowers**, but they still make **seeds**. Conifers have **cones** instead of flowers. Cones are made up of lots of overlapping scales. There are two kinds of cones: male and female. In most conifers both kinds grow on the same tree. When people talk about "pinecones," they usually mean the female cones, and it is the female cones that carry the seeds.

Male cones are smaller and softer than female cones. They produce and release **pollen**, which is usually **dispersed** by the wind. Female **sex cells** are found on the scales of the large female cones. When pollen lands on the female cones it **fertilizes** the female cells, and seeds start to form.

Conifer seeds do not have **seed coats**, and so they are called naked seeds. They grow between the scales of the female cones for protection. The female cones thicken, darken, and harden as the seeds inside their scales develop and ripen. Some cones, such as Scots pine, change from small and green to large, brown, and tough as the seeds develop.

Kinds of cones

Cones are often smooth and egg-shaped, as on cedar trees, but they can be long and thin, as on spruce. Some cones, such as those on the douglas fir or monkey puzzle tree, have prickly scales. The cones of the sugar pine tree (*Pinus lambertiana*), found in the mountains of the western United States, can grow as long as 26 inches (65 centimeters)!

The female cone on this larch tree (*Larix*) is reddish-brown and woody. The male cone (at the top) is smaller and softer.

When the time is right

When the seeds are ready, the cones release them. Most cones take a year to mature, although pinecones may take three years. Cones release seeds in two different ways. Some, such as pines, open their scales to release the seeds in dry weather. The seeds of Scots pine trees (*Pinus sylvestris*) have a single papery wing that helps them float away from the parent tree. When all the seeds have gone, the cones fall to the ground and gradually rot away.

Other cones, such as those on a cedar tree (*Cedrus*), use a different method. Each cedar scale has two seeds growing on it. When the seeds are ripe, the tip of the cone breaks, and gradually the scales fall off. They drop to the ground with the seeds attached. That is why it is rare to see a whole cedar cone fallen from a tree. In some other conifers, the seeds are released as the scales fall.

Fire power!

The Monterey pine (*Pinus radiata*) has cones that refuse to open for anything but the burning heat of a forest fire. The flames destroy other trees, but the Monterey pine is protected by its thick bark. Its cones finally heat up enough to release their seeds, which fall to the ground. Since few other trees survive the fire, the seeds do not have to compete for light and **nutrients**, which gives them a good chance of **germinating** and growing into new trees.

Spores

Ferns, mosses, liverworts, and **algae** are other types of plants that do not grow **flowers**, but unlike **conifer** trees, they do not make **seeds**, either. These plants **reproduce** in a different way—using **spores**.

Spores are microscopically tiny flecks of living material. When released from the plant, they are able to grow into a clone. A clone is a new plant that is identical to the parent plant. Different types of plants produce spores of different sizes and shapes, but most spores consist of a single **cell**. Spores are so small that they are very hard to see, but they are grouped together in packages called **sporangia**. You may have seen sporangia on the underside of many fern fronds (**leaves**). They look like dimpled brown pinheads.

Plants release their spores when they are ripe. Spores have a thick outer coat that protects them against harsh conditions, which means that they can remain **dormant** for several months or even years until conditions are right for them to develop into new plants. Most moss spores need damp, shady places. Ferns, mosses, algae, and horsetails produce millions of spores to ensure that at least some have a chance of landing in conditions right for growth.

The brown spots on the underside of this fern frond are the sporangia that produce the plant's spores. They hold the spores until they are ready to be released.

Spore containers

Different plants produce sporangia that look very different. Mosses and liverworts are the plants that form velvety green carpets over woodland floors, damp walls, or riverside tree trunks. In spring, mosses produce **stalks** with a small, oval capsule at the tip. Spores grow inside the capsule.

Horsetails (*Equisetum*) make their spores in structures that look like "cones." These grow at the end of tube-like **stems**. The cones of the great horsetail (*Equisetum telmateia*) are several inches long on stems over 3 feet (1 meter) high, surrounded by rings of needle-shaped leaves. Algae make their spores in special places on their fronds. In wakame seaweed (*Undaria pinnatifida*) the sporangia are like little leaves at the base of the frond, but the yellow-brown sporangia of the bladderwrack seaweed (*Fucus vesiculosus*) are at the frond tip.

The sporangia of different **species** of fern have different shapes, too. On bracken (*Pteridium*) they are circular, but on hart's tongue fern (*Phyllitis scolopendrium*) they are like stripes. The sporangia of maidenhair ferns (*Adiantum*) are protected behind little flaps along the edges of the frond.

The capsules on this moss are held shut by a ring of "teeth." In dry weather, when the spores are ripe, the teeth will bend back and the spores will be blown away.

Stems

Stems come in all shapes and sizes. They range from the flimsy green stem of a primrose to the thick brown and woody trunk of a tree. In bamboo, the stem is the largest part of the plant. In others plants such as cabbage, the stem is so short that it appears not to have a stem at all. The stems of many roses are covered in thorns to prevent them from being eaten by animals.

Most stems grow up from the ground. Their job is to hold the **leaves** up to the light so that **photosynthesis** can take place and to hold **flowers** in the best position for **pollination**. A stem's other job is to carry water and food to all parts of the plant. It carries them in tubes. One set of tubes, called the **xylem**, carries water and **nutrients** from the **roots**. Other tubes, called the **phloem**, carry food made in the leaves to the rest of the plant.

Going underground

Most stems grow upright, but some grow partly underground, for protection. They may stay underground or grow sideways through the soil. Swollen stems that grow beneath the ground on potato plants are called **tubers**. The potato tuber is the plant's food store and the part that we eat. On flowering plants such as irises, swollen stems are called **rhizomes**.

This cross-section of a stem shows the tubes that carry water and food to all parts of the plant.

Going up!

Some plants have weak, floppy stems that cannot support themselves. Runners are horizontal stems that grow across the ground. Strawberry runners produce flowers, leaves, and roots at intervals along their length. These form new plants when the runner linking them to the old plant breaks down.

Climbers have floppy stems, but they manage to grow upward. Some, such as morning glory (*Ipomoea*), coil their wiry stems around other plants' stems to help them reach the light. Ivy plants have tiny roots coming out of their stem. These grow into cracks and crevices on walls, anchoring the plant firmly in place.

Some plants, such as pea plants and clematis, send out thin, curly **tendrils**. The tips of tendrils are like long fingers, and they are sensitive to touch. They grow out randomly, and when they touch something they curl around it.

The stems on a wisteria plant twist around poles or wires to support the plant. Then they become thick or woody.

Water power

Many plant stems are quite hard and firm so that they can stand up straight and support the weight of the leaves and flowers. Most plant stems manage to stand up because they are supported by water pressure. The flow of water through the stem helps them to stay upright. When water is scarce, the stem does not get enough to help it stand tall, which is why plants wilt or droop.

Trunks and Branches

Trunks and branches are the **stems** of a tree. Just like the smaller stems of other plants, their job is to hold up **leaves** and **flowers**. The difference is that the tough, thick stems on trees are made of wood. Trunks need to be extra strong because they have to support heavy branches, twigs, and many leaves.

The trunk and branches of a tree are also the places where water, food, and **nutrients** move around. Water and nutrients are taken in from the **roots** and sucked up the trunk and along the branches to all the parts of the tree. At the same time, food, made in the leaves, is carried away from the leaves to the rest of the tree. This movement of food and water goes on constantly, just underneath the layer of bark that wraps itself around the outside of the tree like a skin.

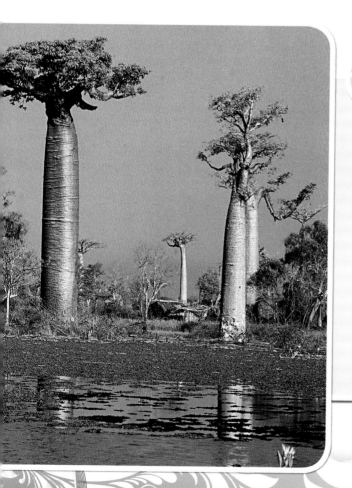

The ballooning baobab tree

The trunk of the African baobab tree (*Adansonia digitata*), unlike most other trunks, swells and slims throughout the year. These strange-looking trees, which grow up to 82 feet (25 meters) tall, have very small branches compared to their wide, thick trunks. In the parts of Africa where they grow, there are long dry spells. When a rainy spell comes, the trunk of the baobab tree fattens up with a huge water store. As this store is used up, the trunk of the baobab tree slims down again!

Inside a trunk

If you look at the cut surface of a log, you will see lots of rings, called **annual rings**, radiating out from the center. Each ring represents one year's growth. To find out how old a tree is, you count the number of annual rings it has in its trunk.

You can also see different layers of wood inside a trunk. The middle part of the trunk is called heartwood. It is made up of dead, woody **cells** that have become very hard. The heartwood helps to make the tree trunk strong. Closer to the surface is a very thin layer made up of living cells. This is the sapwood, where water and nutrients are carried up through the **xylem** from the roots. It is also where **phloem** tubes carry food made by the leaves to the rest of the tree. The outermost layer is the bark, which protects the sapwood beneath it.

By counting the annual rings on a tree, you can tell how many years old it was when it was cut down.

bark

sapwood

heartwood

Rubber trees?

The next time you bounce a rubber ball, think about the tree it came from. Most rubber is made from white latex (**sap**) from rubber trees (*Hevea brasiliensis*). Workers make cuts in the bark and collect the latex that oozes out into cups attached to the tree.

Bark

Bark is like the skin on your body. It is a tough outer layer that covers the main body of the tree—its trunk and branches—and helps protect the parts inside.

Different trees have different sorts of bark, and this can help you identify the tree **species** you are looking at. The bark on a silver birch (*Betula pendula*) is papery and, as its name suggests, is silvery-white in color. The bark of many **coniferous** trees, such as pine trees, flakes off in small, jigsaw puzzle-shaped pieces as the trees grow older. Some trees have distinctive bark patterns, such as the circles on a monkey-puzzle tree (*Araucaria araucana*).

The bark of a tree usually gets thicker as the tree gets older. However, on an ancient beech tree, the bark is thin because older layers flake and drop off. This does not happen to the bark of a redwood tree (*Sequoia sempervirens*), which can be 12 inches (30 centimeters) thick. The redwood's thick bark helps make the tree fire-resistant.

Cracking and splitting

Bark does not stretch as skin does. It cracks, splits, or peels as a tree grows. Younger trees usually have smooth bark. As the tree grows wider, the outer layers of bark on the outside split or peel as newer layers inside push outward.

The reddish color and the curling ends of its outer layer of peeling bark identifies this as a paperbark maple.

The living dead

We all know that trees are living things, but did you know that, apart from the **buds** and **leaves**, the rest of the tree we can see is dead? Bark is made up of two layers. The inner layer that we cannot see is the living, growing part. Every year this special layer of growing **cells** makes a new ring of bark. The new bark pushes the older bark outward. The old bark is cut off from the nourishing fluids moving through the **xylem** and **phloem** tubes in the tree, and it dies. It then becomes part of the visible outer layer of dead bark.

Bark does several very important jobs. It protects the xylem and phloem inside the tree trunk. Bark also protects the tree from damage by insects and **fungi**. If woodland animals, such as deer, chew bark, they leave a hole or wound in the tree. If the wound stays open, insects or fungi damage the live wood underneath. Some trees release a sticky liquid, called **sap**, from their phloem to plug small holes in their bark. This can dry hard and acts a bit like plaster.

Some insects chew softwood, leaving burrows under the bark. If large numbers of insects attack wood in this way, the tree can be damaged.

Roots

The **roots** of a plant are like the foundations of a building. Foundations are built under ground to hold buildings up and bring in pipes and cables carrying water and electricity. Roots anchor a plant firmly in the soil, holding it in place even in high winds. They also take in water and **nutrients** that are essential for the plant's survival.

Soil secrets

In addition to water, people need different types of food to stay healthy, such as the **vitamins** found in fruit. Plants also need different types of nutrients. They make some foods by **photosynthesis**, but they get other nutrients they need from the soil. Useful **minerals** come from the very tiny bits of broken-up rock that form part of the soil. Other nutrients come from dead plant and animal matter that has rotted down to become part of the soil.

Types of roots

Even though most roots do the same jobs, there are many different types, shapes, and sizes. The type of roots a plant has may depend on how large the plant grows and the type of **habitat** it lives in. For example, plants that grow where water is scarce or the soil is poor grow much deeper roots than other plants, in their search for water or nutrients.

Roots have to be strong enough to push their way through tightly packed soil. Some roots even have the strength to damage buildings and rocks. If they grow into cracks in a building, they can eventually split it apart!

How do roots work?

As a root grows, smaller roots branch out from it. The larger roots are tougher, with thicker skins. They help to hold the plant in place. The smallest roots are covered with lots of tiny hairs that have thick skins. These root hairs suck up water and nutrients from the soil. The water and nutrients travel into **xylem** tubes in the larger roots and move up through the **stem** or trunk to the leaves and the rest of the plant.

Under the microscope

Roots in partnership

Members of the pea and clover family have special additions to their roots. These large, round **nodules** are full of **bacteria** (shown in dark blue in this image). The bacteria work together with the plant. They take nitrogen from the air and turn it into nitrates, which the plant needs to grow healthily. In return, the bacteria are safe in the root nodules and supplied with food and water by the plant. Other plants, particularly trees, can form a root partnership known as mycorrhizae with **fungi**. The fungi help the plants to take up huge amounts of water and minerals from the soil and in return get food from the plant.

Types of Roots

There are two main types of **roots**: fibrous roots and taproots. Plants with many roots, all of which are roughly the same size, are said to have fibrous roots. The many roots spread out in all directions under the ground, but they do not go very deeply into the soil. Plants that have fibrous roots include grasses and many trees. The spread of a tree's roots below ground usually matches the width of its crown (the branches and **leaves** above the trunk).

A plant with a taproot, such as a dandelion, has one root that is bigger than all the rest. This main root grows straight down into the soil. Smaller, thinner roots grow out from the side of it. In some plants with taproots, such as carrots or radishes, the taproot becomes swollen with food made by leaves of the plant. This is the part we eat. The plant stores the food like this so it can use it if conditions change and it is unable to make its own food for a while. Some trees, such as oak and pine trees, have taproots.

This marigold plant grows a main taproot that is larger than the other roots. These smaller roots can grow sideways from the taproot.

Plant parts work together

Each of the plant parts we have looked at in this book is different. The parts look different and they have different jobs to do, but they all work together to form a whole. The roots and leaves supply the plant with the **energy** and **nutrients** it needs. Tubes in these parts and in the **stem** carry water, food, and nutrients throughout the plant. These nourish the plant, enabling it to grow and produce other parts, such as **flowers**, **fruits**, **cones**, and **spores**. These, in turn, allow the plant to produce **seeds**, which may grow into new plants to begin the cycle again. A plant is a bit like a human body. It may be made up of separate parts, but the individual parts need to work together if the plant is to live, grow, and thrive.

Remarkable roots

Special **habitats** require special types of roots. In the Amazon **rain forest**, some types of fig trees are over 130 feet (40 meters) tall, but they grow in shallow soil. To prevent them from toppling over, they have wedge-shaped roots above the surface of the ground. These buttress roots grow up the side of the trunks and act like feet, helping the tree to stand firm (see right). In Australian **mangrove** swamps, mangrove plants grow in such thick, wet mud that their roots cannot get the air they need. So, they produce some roots that grow upward out of the water into the air.

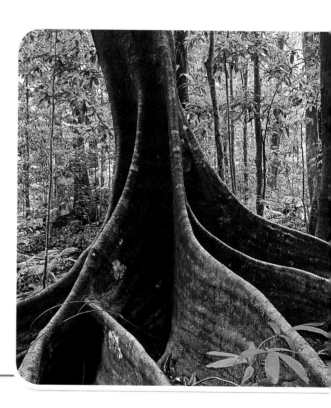

Try It Yourself!

Try these experiments and activities to find out more about some of the plant parts you have explored in this book.

Flower power!

You can make a **flower** any color you like by using the power in its **stem**.

You will need:

- Two glasses
- Water
- Two white flowers (carnations are ideal)
- Blue and red food coloring (or inks)

Cut 2 inches (5 centimeters) off the bottom of each of the flower stems. Look at the cut end. Can you see any tubes?

Fill one glass halfway with water and add a few drops of red coloring. Fill the second glass halfway with water and add a few drops of blue coloring.

Stand one flower in each glass. Leave it for a day.

What happens? Your white flowers should change color. As the stem has taken up water from its base to the flower, it has also taken up the food coloring. The food coloring has dyed the **petals** a different color.

Bark rubbings

Taking bark rubbings is fun, and it is a great way to examine the different kinds of bark patterns trees have.

You will need:

- A pencil
- Brown crayons
- Large sheets of paper

Hold a sheet of paper against the bark of a tree. You may need a friend to hold it for you. Rub the crayon lengthways over the paper, not using the point. Try to cover the whole sheet. Write the name of the tree the rubbing came from on the back of the paper with the pencil.

Repeat this process for different kinds of trees.

You could put your rubbings in a scrapbook or make a display of them, with labels telling people which kinds of trees they came from.

Hyacinth happenings

When you grow a hyacinth **bulb** in a glass jar, it is easy to see the **roots** that grow from it.

You will need:

- A hyacinth bulb
- A glass jar with a narrow top (which is about the width of the bulb)
- Water
- A magnifying glass

Fill the jar with water to the point where, when the bulb is sitting on the top of the jar, the bottom of the bulb just touches the water. Stand the bulb in the jar and put them in a warm, light spot, such as a windowsill.

When roots begin to grow from the bulb, take the magnifying glass and look closely at them. You should be able to see the root hairs growing out from the roots.

These root hairs help the roots cover an even wider area as they reach out to collect water for the plant.

If you continue to take care of your plant, keeping the water supply topped up, it should produce a colorful, scented flower after a few weeks.

Plant parts we can eat!

Have you ever really thought about which part of a plant you are eating when you munch on **fruits** or vegetables?

You will need:

- A notepad
- A pencil
- An adult to take you to a supermarket

Look at all the different fruits and vegetables in the supermarket and try to identify which part of the plant they are or come from. You could make your findings into a chart. You could use the headings "Type of food," under which you would put entries such as broccoli and celery, and "Part of plant," under which you would include flower and stem.

Looking at Plant Parts

Naming plant parts

This diagram of a plant reminds you of the parts that most plants have in common and what those parts do.

Flowers are the plant's **reproductive** part. They make **seeds**, which may grow into new plants, like the parent plant.

Buds hold tiny **leaves** or flowers until the time is right for them to open up.

Fruits protect the seeds as they grow and help to **disperse** the seeds away from the parent plant so that the seeds have a better chance of growing.

Seeds are made in the flowers. When they land in a suitable spot they grow into new plants.

Leaves are the food factories of the plant. Leaves collect sunlight, which they use to convert water and **carbon dioxide** into food.

The **stem** holds the other parts of the plant up. It holds the leaves up to collect sunlight and the flowers up so insects or wind can help them disperse their **pollen** and seeds.

Roots anchor the plant in the ground and take in water and **nutrients** through root hairs. Root hairs are usually too tiny to see.

Leaf shapes

Simple leaves

Ivy (*Hedera helix*)

Olive (*Osmanthus americanus*)

Pacific dogwood (*Cornus nuttallii*)

Toothed simple leaves

Holly (*Ilex*)

White alder (*Alnus rhombifolia*)

Sweet chestnut (*Castanea sativa*)

Simple strap-like leaves

Tulip (*Tulipa*)

Bamboo (*Arundinaria*)

Iris (*Iris*)

Lobed simple leaves

Sycamore (*Acer pseudoplatanus*)

Sugar maple (*Acer saccharum*)

California scrub oak (*Quercus dumosa*)

Needles and spines

Scots pine (*Pinus sylvestris*)

Redwood (*Sequoia sempervirens*)

Giant sequoia (*Sequoiadendron giganteum*)

Australian pine (*Casuarina equisetifolia*)

Compound leaves

Ash (*Fraxinus*)

Horse chestnut (*Aesculus*)

Pear tree (*Caragana*)

Coconut palm (*Cocos nucifera*)

Arrangements of flowers

Simple flowers

Carnation (*Dianthus*)

Iris (*Iris*)

Oriental poppy (*Papaver*)

Tulip (*Tulipa*)

Buttercup (*Ranunculus*)

Umbel

Umbels have umbrella-like arrangements of flowers. At the end of a stem are flower stalks of equal length, each with a single flower or tiny group of flowers at the end. The flowers may be held up or down.

Flowering garlic (*Allium*)

Giant hogweed (*Heracleum*)

Angelica (*Angelica*)

Leafy spurge (*Euphorbia esula*)

Composites—flower clusters

Composites look like a single flower, but the flower head is actually made of hundreds of tiny flowers packed closely together.

Ox-eye daisy (*Telekia*)

Sunflower (*Helianthus*)

Clover (*Trifolium*)

Edelweiss (*Leontopodium*)

Spike

Lots of flowers grow from a stem, each on their own little **stalk**. The oldest flower is at the bottom, the youngest at the top.

Foxglove (Digitalis)

Yucca (*Yucca*)

Orchid (*Orchis*)

Pampas grass (*Cortaderia*)

Glossary

algae group of plants that do not have leaves, stems, roots, or flowers. We call them plants because they can use sunlight to make their own food in the process of photosynthesis.

annual ring ring you can see when the trunk of a tree is cut down. If you count annual rings, you can find out how old a tree is.

anther swollen tip of a stamen, the male reproductive parts of a flower. Each anther is made up of pollen sacs, which contain grains of pollen.

bacteria tiny organisms in the soil, water, and air

blade flat part of the leaf

bud swelling on a plant stem of tiny, young, overlapping leaves or petals and other flower parts, ready to burst into bloom

bulb underground bud protected by layers of thick, fleshy leaves. An onion is a type of bulb.

carbon dioxide gas in the air around us that plants use for photosynthesis

carpel name for the female parts of a flower. The ovary, style, and stigma together make up a carpel.

cell building block of living things, so small it can only be seen with a microscope. Some microbes consist of a single cell, but most plants and animals are made up of millions or billions of cells.

chlorophyll green substance found in plants that is used in photosynthesis. Chlorophyll gives leaves their green color.

cluster group of flowers growing together

cone form of dry fruit (in which seeds develop) produced by conifer trees. Cones are often egg-shaped, and they are made up of loads of overlapping scales in which seeds grow.

conifer/coniferous type of tree that has cones and needle-like leaves

deciduous type of tree that loses all its leaves in winter. In cool climates, deciduous trees lose their leaves before winter, but in tropical areas there are deciduous trees that lose their leaves at the start of the dry season.

disperse scatter in different directions. The main methods of seed dispersal are by wind, water, or animal.

dormant describes a living thing that is resting before growing

embryo very young plant that is contained in a seed

energy all living things need energy in order to live and grow

evaporate/evaporation when water turns from liquid into a vapor (a gas). When clothes dry on a clothes line, it is because the water evaporates and the vapor becomes part of the air.

fat nutrient that gives living things energy

fertilize/fertilization when one flower's male sex cell joins with another flower's female sex cell and begins to form a seed

flower reproductive parts of a plant. Flowers contain the parts that can make seeds.

fungi group of living things that are plant-like but do not contain chlorophyll (and are therefore unable to use photosynthesis to make their own food). Toadstools and mushrooms are types of fungi.

germinate/germination when a seed starts to grow

habitat place where plants (and animals) live

inflorescence flower-like head that is made up of lots of tiny flowers (florets) growing closely together

leaf plant part that makes the plant's food

mangrove type of plant that grows in seashore mud

midrib central vein that runs up through the middle of a leaf

mineral chemical building block of rocks. Plants need some minerals in order to grow and reproduce.

nectar sugary substance plants make to attract insects, which like to eat it

nectary place at the base of flower petals where nectar is made and stored

nodule small swelling found on the roots of some plants. It contains bacteria that helps the plant to absorb nitrogen.

nutrient chemical that plants and animals need in order to live

organism living thing, such as a bacterium, cell, plant, or animal

ovary part of the flower that contains the female sex cells. It forms the bottom part of the carpel.

petal colored part of a flower

petiole stalk that attaches a leaf to a stem

phloem tubes that carry food (sugars) made in the leaf to all the other parts of the plant

photosynthesis process by which plants make their own food using water, carbon dioxide (a gas in the air), and energy from sunlight

pigment natural substance that gives color. Leaves are green because they contain a green pigment called chlorophyll.

pod capsule that holds the seeds of legume plants, such as peas

pollen tiny dust-like particles that are produced by the anthers in the male part of a flower

pollinate/pollination when pollen travels from the anthers of one flower to the stigma of the same or a different flower

protein protein is needed by living things for growth, maintenance, and repair of their bodies

rain forest kind of forest habitat that exists in very hot and wet (rainy) countries of the world

receptacle swollen end of the flower nearest to the stem

reproduce/reproduction when a living thing produces young like itself

rhizome special type of stem that grows under the ground instead of up in the air

root plant part that anchors plants firmly in the ground and takes in water and nutrients

sap sugary liquid containing food made in the leaves. Sap flows in a plant's phloem tubes.

seed part of a plant that contains the beginnings of a new plant

seed coat tough, outer skin of a seed that protects the tiny new plant inside that is waiting to grow

seed leaf leaf that stores food inside a seed. The young plant inside a seed uses the food to provide the energy it needs to grow.

sepal green petal-like structure. Sepals protect the inner parts of a bud until the bud is ready to open.

sex cell special male or female cells that combine to make an embryo. Male sex cells are called sperm, and female sex cells are called ovules.

shoot new stem growing from the main stem of a plant or out of a seed

species type of living thing. Organisms of the same species can breed together to produce offspring.

sporangia sacs or capsules containing groups of spores

spore tiny particle, usually containing a single cell, that can grow into a new plant

stalk part of the plant that attaches the leaf to the stem. Flower stalks attach little flowers to a stem.

stamen male reproductive part of a flower that produces pollen

stem part of the plant that holds it upright and supports its leaves and flowers

stomata (singular is **stoma**) tiny openings on a leaf, usually on the underside. They help a plant to take in air and also prevent too much water from escaping when it is hot.

tendril very long, thin leaf that wraps around supports to hold up a climbing plant

tuber stem that grows underground and becomes swollen with the food that the plant stores inside it. Potatoes are a type of tuber.

umbel group of small flowers that form an umbrella-like shape

vein tiny tube that helps support a leaf. Xylem and phloem tubes run through the veins, carrying water to the leaves and food made in the leaves to other parts of the plant.

vitamin type of nutrient in food that helps animals grow and protects them from illness

xylem tubes in a plant that carry water and nutrients from the roots to all the other parts of the plant

Further Information

Books

Burnie, David. *The Concise Nature Encyclopedia.* Boston: Kingfisher, 2006.

Burnie, David. *Eyewitness Guide: Tree.* New York: Dorling Kindersley, 2005.

Casper, Julie Kerr. *Natural Resources: Plants.* New York: Chelsea House, 2007.

Hipp, Andrew. *The Green World: Plant Diversity.* New York: Chelsea House, 2007.

Parker, Edward. *Rain forests: Trees and Plants.* Chicago: Raintree, 2003.

Riley, Peter. *Everyday Science: Plants.* Milwaukee: Gareth Stevens, 2004.

Silverstein, Alvin, Virginia Silverstein, and Laura Silverstein Nunn. *Science Concepts Second: Photosynthesis.* Brookfield, Conn.: Twenty-First Century Books, 2007.

Websites

www.mbgnet.net
At Missouri Botanical Garden's website, you can compare the habitats of the world.

www.kew.org/plants/titan/index.html
See the opening of the titan arum bud as well as lots of interesting information about one of the world's smelliest flowers.

www.urbanext.uiuc.edu/gpe/gpe.html
"The Great Plant Escape" is a fun way of learning about what different plant parts do. There is also a simple glossary of terms.

Conservation sites

These sites provide information on the dangers to wild plants and habitats and what conservation groups are doing to help them survive.

www.panda.org
The Worldwide Wildlife Fund works to protect animals and habitats.

www.sierraclub.org
The Sierra Club website provides information about the preservation work carried out by the group.

Places to visit

Many museums, arboretums (botanical gardens devoted to trees), and botanic gardens are fascinating places to visit. You could try:

United States Botanic Garden
245 First Street, S.W.
Washington, DC 20024
www.usbg.gov

New York Botanical Garden
Bronx River Parkway at Fordham Road
Bronx, NY 10458
www.nybg.org

Chicago Botanic Garden
1000 Lake Cook Road
Glencoe, IL 60022
www.chicagobotanic.org

Los Angeles County Arboretum & Botanic Garden
301 North Baldwin Avenue
Arcadia, CA 91007
www.arboretum.org

The State Botanical Garden of Georgia
2450 South Milledge Avenue
Athens, Georgia 30605
www.uga.edu/botgarden

You can also find out about plants by visiting local garden centers. The Latin names of plants will be on the plants' labels, so you can try to find as many related plants as you can.

Index